TO
THE LAND
OF
NURSERY
RHYME
—
I SMILE

OLD KING COLE WAS A MERRY OLD SOUL

ii

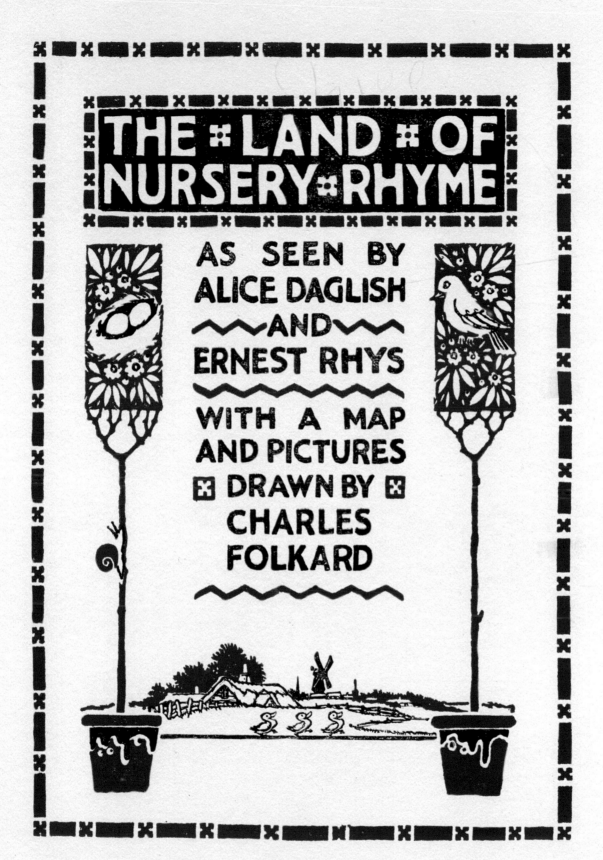

THE LAND OF NURSERY RHYME

AS SEEN BY ALICE DAGLISH AND ERNEST RHYS

WITH A MAP AND PICTURES DRAWN BY CHARLES FOLKARD

This edition produced for The Book People Ltd, Hall Wood Avenue,
Haydock, St Helens WA11 9UL

This edition first published in Great Britain in 2008
by Orion Books
5 Upper St Martin's Lane
London
WC2H 9EA

Rhymes and illustrations selected in 2008 by Orion Books from
The Land of Nursery Rhyme, first published in 1932 by J.M. Dent & Sons.
Designed by jetdesigns.co.uk

A CIP catalogue record for this book is available from the
British Library.

ISBN 978-1-4072-1456-6

Printed and bound in Spain by Graficas Estella

The Orion Publishing Group's policy is to use papers that are natural,
renewable and recyclable products and made from wood grown in
sustainable forests. The logging and manufacturing processes are expected
to conform to the environmental regulations of the country of origin.

www.orionbooks.co.uk

INTRODUCTION

DEAR CHILDREN,

Here are the favourite old Nursery Rhymes. No doubt you who read these pages may be tempted to try making up some fresh ones. Because, you know, that is how the old rhymes first began. As the proverb says: 'One song leads to another', and when one story is ended, another one begins! So there can be no harm in your thinking of more rhymes for yourselves, or even perhaps, what is still better, making fresh pictures for some of the pages that the artist has not already illustrated. The Land of Nursery Rhyme lies very near to Fairyland, and when you go out of one gate you can easily go into the other.

A.D.
E.R.

☀LIST ☀☀ OF ☀☀ ADDRESSES☀

THE LAND OF

·NURSERY RHYME

LITTLE BOY BLUE

Little Boy Blue, come blow your horn,
The sheep's in the meadow, the cow's in the corn;
But where is the boy that looks after the sheep?
He's under a haystack, fast asleep.
Will you wake him? No, not I;
For if I do, he'll surely cry.

RED SKY AT NIGHT

Red sky at night,
    Shepherd's delight.
Red sky in the morning,
    Shepherd's warning.

DING, DONG, BELL

Ding, dong, bell,
    Pussy's in the well.
        Who put her in?
            Little Tommy Green.
        Who pulled her out?
Little Tommy Trout.
    What a naughty boy was that,
        To drown a little pussy cat
Who never did him any harm,
But killed all the mice in his father's barn!

A CAT MAY LOOK AT A KING

A cat may look at a King,
And sure I may look at an ugly thing.

THIRTY DAYS HATH SEPTEMBER

Thirty days hath September,
April, June and November;
February has twenty-eight alone,
All the rest have thirty-one,
Excepting leap-year, that's the time
When February's days are twenty-nine.

SLEEPY HARRY

'I do not like to go to bed,'
Sleepy little Harry said;
'So, naughty Betty, go away,
I will not come at all, I say.'

Oh, what a silly little fellow!
I should be quite ashamed to tell her;
Betty, you must come and carry
This very foolish little Harry.

The little birds are better taught,
They go roosting when they ought;
And all the ducks and fowls, you know,
THEY went to bed an hour ago.

TWEEDLE-DUM AND TWEEDLE-DEE

Tweedle-Dum and Tweedle-Dee
  Resolved to have a battle,
For Tweedle-Dum said Tweedle-Dee
  Had spoiled his nice new rattle.
Just then flew by a monstrous crow,
  As big as a tar-barrel,
Which frightened both the heroes so,
  They quite forgot their quarrel.

THERE WAS A LITTLE GUINEA-PIG

There was a little guinea-pig
Who, being little, was not big;
He always walked upon his feet,
And never fasted when he eat.

When from a place he ran away,
He never at that place did stay;
And while he ran, as I am told,
He ne'er stood still for young or old.

He often squeaked, and sometimes
violent,
And when he squeaked he ne'er was
silent.
Though ne'er instructed by a cat,
He knew a mouse was not a rat.

One day, as I am certified,
He took a whim and fairly died;
And as I am told by men of sense,
He never has been living since.

BOW-WOW, SAYS THE DOG

Bow-wow, says the dog;
  Mew, mew, says the cat;
Grunt, grunt, goes the hog;
  And squeak, goes the rat.

Tu-whu, says the owl;
  Caw, caw, says the crow;
Quack, quack, says the duck;
  And moo, says the cow.

THERE WAS A RAT

There was a rat, for want of stairs,
Went down a rope to say his prayers.

BABY

Where did you come from, baby dear?
  Out of the everywhere into here.

Where did you get those eyes of blue?
  Out of the sky as I came through.

What makes the light in them sparkle and spin?
  Some of the starry twinkles left in.

Where did you get that little tear?
  I found it waiting when I got here.

What makes your forehead so smooth and high?
  A soft hand stroked it as I went by.

What makes your cheek like a warm white rose?
  I saw something better than anyone knows.

Whence that three-cornered smile of bliss?
  Three angels gave me at once a kiss.

When did you get this pearly ear?
  God spoke, and it came out to hear.

How did they all just come to be you?
  God thought about me, and so I grew.

But how did you come to us, you dear?
  God thought about you, and so I am here!

HUMPTY DUMPTY

Humpty Dumpty sat on a wall,
Humpty Dumpty had a great fall;
All the King's horses and all the King's men
Couldn't put Humpty together again.

GOLDEN SLUMBERS

Golden slumbers kiss your eyes,
Smiles awake you when you rise.
Sleep, pretty children; do not cry,
And I will sing a lullaby:
Rock them, rock them, lullaby.

Care is heavy, therefore sleep you;
You are care, and care must keep you.
Sleep, pretty children; do not cry,
And I will sing a lullaby:
Rock them, rock them, lullaby.

THE TURTLE-DOVE'S NEST

High in the pine-tree
  The little turtle-dove
Made a little nursery,
  To please her little love.
'Coo', said the little turtle-dove,
  'Coo', said she;
In the long shady branches
  Of the dark pine-tree.

A CANDLE

Little Nancy Etticoat,
  In a white petticoat,
    And a red nose;
      The longer she stands,
        The shorter she grows.

WHEN THE WIND IS IN THE EAST

When the wind is in the east,
'Tis neither good for man nor beast;
When the wind is in the north,
The skilful fisher goes not forth;
When the wind is in the south,
It blows the bait in the fishes' mouth;
When the wind is in the west,
Then 'tis at the very best.

SNEEZE ON MONDAY

Sneeze on Monday, sneeze for danger;
Sneeze on Tuesday, kiss a stranger;
Sneeze on Wednesday, get a letter;
Sneeze on Thursday, something better;
Sneeze on Friday, sneeze for sorrow;
Sneeze on Saturday, see your sweetheart tomorrow.

LOOBY LOO

Here we dance Looby Loo,
Here we dance Looby light,
Here we dance Looby Loo,
Dance with all your might.
Put your right hand in, put your right hand out,
Shake yourself a little, and turn yourself about.

DANCE TO YOUR DADDY

Dance to your daddy,
My little babby;
Dance to your daddy;
My little lamb.
You shall have a fishy
In a little dishy;
You shall have a fishy,
When the boat comes in.

HOW DOTH THE LITTLE CROCODILE

How doth the little crocodile
  Improve his shining tail,
And pour the waters of the Nile
  On every golden scale!

How cheerfully he seems to grin,
  How neatly spread his claws,
And welcomes little fishes in
  With gently smiling jaws!

WHAT ARE LITTLE BOYS MADE OF?

What are little boys made of, made of?
What are little boys made of?
Slugs and snails, and puppy-dogs' tails;
And that's what little boys are made of, made of.

What are little girls made of, made of?
What are little girls made of?
Sugar and spice, and all that's nice;
And that's what little girls are made of, made of.

BOBBIE SHAFTOE'S GONE TO SEA

Bobbie Shaftoe's gone to sea,
Silver buckles at his knee;
When he comes back, he'll marry me,
Bonny Bobbie Shaftoe!

THE SOUTH WIND BRINGS WET WEATHER

The south wind brings wet weather,
The north wind wet and cold together;
The west wind always brings us rain,
The east wind blows it back again.

MULTIPLICATION IS VEXATION

Multiplication is vexation,
  Division is as bad;
The Rule of Three doth puzzle me,
  And practice drives me mad.

TELL-TALE TIT

Tell-tale tit!
Your tongue shall be slit,
And all the dogs in the town
Shall have a little bit.

I Had A Little Doggy

I had a little doggy
that used to sit and beg;
But doggy tumbled down the stairs
and broke his little leg.

Oh, doggy, I will nurse you,
and try to make you well,
And you shall have a collar
with a little silver bell.

Ah, doggy, don't you think
that you should very faithful be,
For having such a loving friend
to comfort you as me?

And when your leg is better,
and you can run and play,
We'll have a scamper in the fields
and see them making hay.

But, doggy, you must promise
(and mind your word you keep)
Not once to tease the little lambs,
or run among the sheep;

And then the little yellow chicks
that play upon the grass,
You must not even wag your tail
to scare them as you pass.

THE BABES IN THE WOOD

My dear, do you know
How, a long time ago,
Two poor little children,
Whose names I don't know,

Were stolen away
On a fine summer's day,
And left in a wood,
As I've heard people say?

And when it was night,
So sad was their plight,
The sun it went down,
And the moon gave no light!

They sobbed and they sigh'd,
And they bitterly cried,
And the poor little things
They lay down and died.

And when they were dead,
The robins so red
Brought strawberry leaves
And over them spread;

And all the day long
They sang them this song,
Poor babes in the wood!
Poor babes in the wood!
And don't you remember
The babes in the wood?

THE LOST DOLL

I once had a sweet little doll, dears,
  The prettiest doll in the world,
Her cheeks were so red and so white, dears,
  And her hair was so charmingly curled.
I lost my poor little doll, dears,
  As I played in the heath one day,
And I cried for her more than a week, dears,
  But I never could find where she lay.

I found my poor little doll, dears,
  As I played in the heath one day;
Folk say she is terribly changed, dears,
  For her paint is all washed away,
And her arm trodden off by the cows, dears,
  And her hair not the least bit curled,
Yet for old sake's sake she is still, dears,
  The prettiest doll in the world!

18

NUTS IN MAY

Here we come gathering nuts in May,
   Nuts in May, nuts in May;
Here we come gathering nuts in May,
   On a fine and frosty morning.

Pray who will you gather for nuts in May,
   Nuts in May, nuts in May;
Pray who will you gather for nuts in May,
   On a fine and frosty morning?

We'll gather [name] for nuts in May,
   Nuts in May, nuts in May;
We'll gather [name] for nuts in May,
   On a fine and frosty morning.

Who'll you send to take her away,
   Take her away, take her away;
Pray who'll you send to take her away,
   On a fine and frosty morning?

We'll send [name] to take her away,
   Take her away, take her away;
We'll send [name] to take her away,
   On a fine and frosty morning.

LITTLE BO-PEEP

Little Bo-Peep has lost her sheep,
  And can't tell where to find them;
Leave them alone and they'll come home,
  And bring their tails behind them.

Little Bo-Peep fell fast asleep,
  And dreamt she heard them bleating;
But when she awoke, she found it a joke,
  For they were still a-fleeting.

Then up she took her little crook,
  Determined for to find them;
She found them indeed, but it made her heart bleed,
  For they'd left their tails behind them.

It happened one day, as Bo-Beep did stray
  Unto a meadow hard by:
There she espied their tails side by side,
  All hung on a tree to dry.

Then she heaved a sigh, and wiped her eye,
  And ran o'er hill and dale-o,
And tried what she could, as a shepherdess should,
  To tack to each sheep its tail-o.

LITTLE BO-PEEP

HAS LOST HER SHEEP

21

There Was An Old Woman Lived Under A Hill

There was an old woman lived under a hill;
And if she's not gone, she lives there still.
Baked apples she sold, and cranberry pies,
And she's the old woman who never told lies.

If 'Ifs' And 'Ans'

If 'ifs' and 'ans'
were pots and pans
There'd be no need for tinkers!

ST IVES

As I was going to St Ives,
I met a man with seven wives,
Every wife had seven sacks,
Every sack had seven cats,
Every cat had seven kits:
Kits, cats, sacks, and wives,
How many were there going to St Ives?

I HAD A LITTLE PONY

I had a little pony,
  His name was Dapple-Grey,
I lent him to a lady,
  To ride a mile away;
She whipped him, she lashed him,
  She rode him through the mire;
I would not lend my pony now
  For all the lady's hire.

GIRLS AND BOYS

Girls and boys come out to play,
The moon doth shine as bright as day.
Come with a whoop and come with a call,
Come with good will or not at all.

Leave your supper and leave your sleep,
Come to your playfellows in the street.
Up the ladder and down the wall,
A halfpenny loaf will serve you all.

THE THREE LITTLE KITTENS

THERE were three little kittens
  Put on their mittens,
To eat some Christmas Pie.
  Miaw wow! Miaw wow! Miaw! Miaw! Miaw!

These three little kittens
  They lost their mittens,
And they began to cry:
  Miaw! Miaw! Miaw! Miaw! Miaw!

Go, naughty kittens,
  And find your mittens,
Or you shan't have any pie!
  Miaw! Miaw! Miaw! Miaw! Miaw!

These three little kittens
  They found their mittens,
And joyfully did cry:
  Miaw! Miaw! Miaw! Miaw! Miaw!

Oh, Granny dear,
  Our mittens are here,
Make haste and cut up the pie.
  Purr-rr—rr! purr-rr! Purr-rr!

There Was A Little Girl

There was a little girl and she had a little curl,
Right down the middle of her forehead;
And when she was good, she was very, very good,
But when she was bad, she was horrid.

Rain, Rain, Go Away

Rain, rain, go away,
Come again another day;
Tommy Piper wants to play.

THE QUEEN OF HEARTS

The Queen of Hearts, she made some tarts,
  All on a summer's day;
The Knave of Hearts, he stole the tarts,
  And took them clean away.

The King of Hearts called for the tarts,
  And beat the Knave full sore;
The Knave of Hearts brought back the tarts,
  And vowed he'd steal no more.

THE QUEEN OF HEARTS
SHE MADE SOME TARTS

MARY, MARY

Mary, Mary, quite contrary,
  How does your garden grow?
With cockle shells, and silver bells,
  And pretty maids all in a row, row, row,
And pretty maids all in a row.

THE·HOUSE·THAT·JACK·BUILT

This is the house that Jack built.

This is the malt
That lay in the house
    that Jack built.

This is the rat
That ate the malt
That lay in the house
    that Jack built.

This is the cat
That killed the rat
That ate the malt
That lay in the house
    that Jack built.

This is the dog
That worried the cat,
That killed the rat,
That ate the malt
That lay in the house
    that Jack built.

This is the cow with the
   crumpled horn
That tossed the dog,
That worried the cat,
That killed the rat,
That ate the malt
That lay in the house
   That Jack built.

This is the maiden all forlorn
That milked the cow with the
crumpled horn
That tossed the dog,
That worried the cat,
That killed the rat,
That ate the malt
That lay in the house
   That Jack built.

This is the man all tattered and torn
That kissed the maiden all
   forlorn,
That milked the cow with a
   crumpled horn,
That tossed the dog,
That worried the cat,
That killed the rat
That ate the malt
That lay in the house
   That Jack built.

This is the priest all shaven and shorn
That married the man all tattered and torn,
That kissed the maiden all forlorn,
That milked the cow with a crumpled horn,

That tossed the dog,
That worried the cat,
That killed the rat
That ate the malt
That lay in the house
    That Jack built.

This is the cock that crowed in the morn
That woke the priest all shaven and shorn,
That married the man all tattered and torn,
That kissed the maiden all forlorn,
That milked the cow with
    the crumpled horn,
That tossed the dog,
That worried the cat,
That killed the rat,
That ate the malt
That lay in the house
    That Jack built.

This is the farmer sowing his corn
That kept the cock that crowed in the morn,
That woke the priest all shaven and shorn,
That married the man all tattered and torn,
That kissed the maiden all forlorn,
That milked the cow with
    the crumpled horn,
That tossed the dog,
That worried the cat,
That killed the rat,
That ate the malt
That lay in the house
    That Jack built.

TOM, TOM, THE PIPER'S SON

Tom, Tom, the piper's son,
He learned to play when he was young,
But the only tune that he could play
Was 'Over the hills and far away.'

Now, Tom with his pipe made such a noise,
That he pleased both girls and boys,
And they all stopped to hear him play
'Over the hills and far away.'

Tom, Tom, the piper's son,
Stole a pig, and away he run.
The pig was eat, and Tom was beat,
And Tom went roaring down the street.

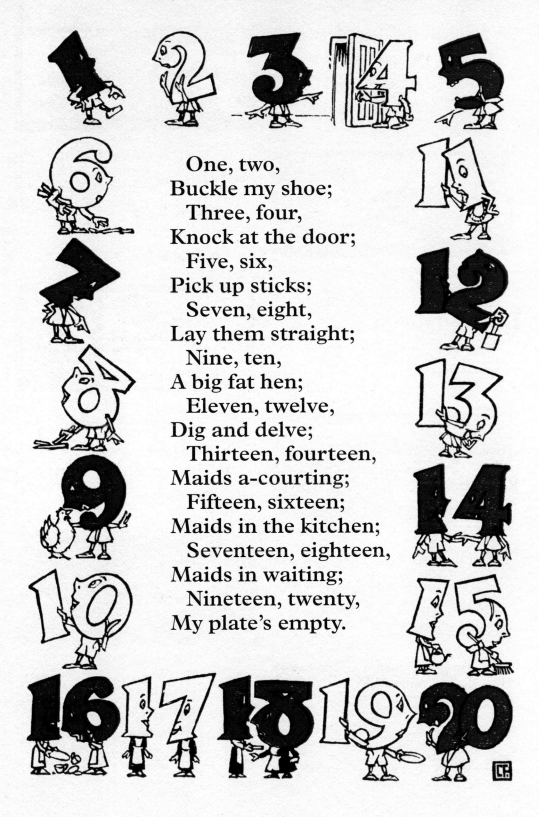

One, two,
Buckle my shoe;
  Three, four,
Knock at the door;
  Five, six,
Pick up sticks;
  Seven, eight,
Lay them straight;
  Nine, ten,
A big fat hen;
  Eleven, twelve,
Dig and delve;
  Thirteen, fourteen,
Maids a-courting;
  Fifteen, sixteen;
Maids in the kitchen;
  Seventeen, eighteen,
Maids in waiting;
  Nineteen, twenty,
My plate's empty.

COCK ROBIN

Who killed Cock Robin?
  I, said the sparrow,
  With my bow and arrow
I killed Cock Robin.

CHORUS:
All the birds in the air
  Fell a'sighing and a'sobbing
When they heard of the death
  Of poor Cock Robin.

Who saw him die?
  I, said the fly,
  With my little eye
I saw him die.

Who caught his blood?
  I, said the fish,
  With my little dish
I caught his blood.

Who'll toll the bell?
  I, said the bull,
  Because I can pull
I'll toll the bell.

Who'll dig his grave?
  I, said the owl,
  With my little trowel
I'll dig his grave.

Who'll be the parson?
I, said the rook,
With my little book
I'll be the parson.

Who'll be chief mourner?
I, said the dove,
For I mourn my love;
I'll be chief mourner.

THE COCK DOTH CROW

The cock doth crow
To let thee know,
An' thou be wise,
'Tis time to rise.

EARLY TO BED

Early to bed,
Early to rise,
Is the way to be healthy,
Wealthy and wise.

MARY HAD A LITTLE LAMB

Mary had a little lamb,
  Its fleece was white as snow;
And everywhere that Mary went
  The lamb was sure to go.

He followed her to school one day;
  That was against the rule;
It made the children laugh and play
  To see a lamb at school.

And so the teacher turned him out,
  But still he lingered near,
And waited patiently about
  Till Mary did appear.

Then he ran to her, and laid
  His head upon her arm,
As if he said, 'I'm not afraid,—
  You'll keep me from all harm.'

'What makes the lamb love Mary so?'
  The eager children cry.
'Oh, Mary loves the lamb, you know,'
  The teacher did reply.

And you each gentle animal
  In confidence may bind,
And make them follow at your call
  If you are always kind.

·AND·EVERYWHERE·THAT·MARY·WENT·
·THE·LAMB·WAS·SURE·TO·GO·

BYE, BABY BUNTING

Bye, baby bunting,
Father's gone a-hunting,
To fetch a little rabbit-skin
To wrap the baby bunting in.

PETER WHITE

Peter White would ne'er go right,
   Would you know the reason why?
He follows his nose wherever he goes,
   And that stands all awry.

SEE-SAW, MARGERY DAW

See-saw, Margery Daw,
   Johnny shall have a new master;
Johnny shall have but a penny a day,
   Because he can't work any faster.

FINGERNAILS

Cut them on Monday, you cut them for health;
Cut them on Tuesday, you cut them for wealth;
Cut them on Wednesday, you cut them for news;
Cut them on Thursday, a new pair of shoes;
Cut them on Friday, you cut them for sorrow;
Cut them on Saturday, see your true love
   tomorrow;
Cut them on Sunday, ill luck will be with you all
   the week.

THE FIVE LITTLE PIGS

(said while holding up each of a child's five toes in
turn from the big toe to the little, ending with
tickling the child under the arms)

This little pig went to the market;

This little pig stayed home;

This little pig got roast beef;

This little pig got none;

This little pig cried,
'Wee, wee, wee',
All the way home.

yes

A man of words and not of deeds
Is like a garden full of weeds;
And when the weeds begin to grow,
It's like a garden full of snow;
And when the snow begins to fall,
It's like a bird upon the wall;
And when the bird away does fly,
It's like an eagle in the sky;
And when the sky begins to roar,
It's like a lion at the door;
And when the door begins to crack,
It's like a stick across your back;
And when your back begins to smart,
It's like a pain within your heart;
And when your heart begins to bleed,
You're dead, and dead, and dead indeed.

PUSSYCAT, PUSSYCAT

Pussycat, pussycat, where have you been?
I've been to London to look at the Queen.
Pussycat, pussycat, what did you there?
I frightened a little mouse under the chair.

POLLY, PUT THE KETTLE ON

Polly, put the kettle on,
Polly, put the kettle on,
Polly, put the kettle on,
We'll all have tea.

Suky, take it off again,
Suky, take it off again,
Suky, take it off again,
     They've all gone away.

LITTLE TOMMY TUCKER

Little Tommy Tucker
     Sang for his supper:
What shall he eat?
     White bread and butter.
How shall he cut it
     Without e'er a knife?
How can he marry
     Without e'er a wife?

There Was A Little Boy And A Little Girl

There was a little boy and a little girl
  Lived in an alley;
Says the little boy to the little girl,
  'Shall I, oh! Shall I?'

Says the little girl to the little boy,
  'What shall we do?'
Says the little boy to the little girl,
  'I will kiss you.'

Georgie Porgie

Georgie Porgie, pudding and pie,
Kissed the girls and made them cry.
When the boys came out to play,
Georgie Porgie ran away.

TWINKLE, TWINKLE

Twinkle, twinkle, little star,
How I wonder what you are!
Up above the world so high,
Like a diamond in the sky!

When the blazing sun is gone,
When he nothing shines upon,
Then you show your little light,
Twinkle, twinkle, all the night.

BLOW, WIND, BLOW

Blow, wind, blow, and go, mill, go,
That the miller may grind his corn;
That the baker may take it,
And into bread make it,
And bring us a loaf in the morn.

THE CAT HAS ATE THE PUDDING-STRING

Sing, sing, what shall I sing?
The cat has ate the pudding-string!
Do, do, what shall I do?
The cat has bit it quite in two.

OLD KING COLE

Old King Cole
Was a merry old soul,
And a merry old soul was he;
He called for his pipe,
And he called for his bowl,
And he called for his fiddlers three.
Every fiddler, he had a fiddle,
And a very fine fiddle had he;
Twee tweedle dee, tweedle dee, went the fiddlers.
Oh, there's none so rare
As can compare
With King Cole and his fiddlers three.

WHEN FAMED KING ARTHUR RULED THIS LAND

When famed King Arthur ruled this land
  He was a goodly king:
He took three pecks of barley meal
  To make a fine pudding.

A rare pudding the king did make,
  And stuffed it well with plums;
And in it are such lumps of fat,
  As big as my two thumbs.

The king and queen did eat thereof,
  And noblemen beside,
And what they could not eat that night
  The queen next morning fried.

A Frog He Would A-Wooing Go

A frog he would a-wooing go,
        Heigho, says Rowley,
Whether his mother would let him or no.
        With a roly poly, gammon and spinach,
        Heigho, says Anthony Rowley!

So off he set with his opera hat,
        Heigho, says Rowley,
And on the road he met with a rat.
        With a roly poly, gammon and spinach,
        Heigho, says Anthony Rowley!

'Pray, Mr Rat, will you go with me,'
        Heigho, says Rowley,
'Kind Mrs Mousey for to see?'
        With a roly poly, gammon and spinach,
        Heigho, says Anthony Rowley!

When they came to the door of Mousey's hall,
        Heigho, says Rowley,
They gave a loud knock and they gave a loud call.
        With a roly poly, gammon and spinach,
        Heigho, says Anthony Rowley!

'Pray, Mrs Mouse, are you within?'
    Heigho, says Rowley,
'Oh, yes, kind sirs, I'm sitting to spin.'
    With a roly poly, gammon and spinach,
    Heigho, says Anthony Rowley!

'Pray, Mrs Mouse will you give us some beer?'
    Heigho, says Rowley,
'For froggy and I are fond of good cheer.'
    With a roly poly, gammon and spinach,
    Heigho, says Anthony Rowley!

'Pray Mr Frog, will you give us a song?'
    Heigho, says Rowley,
'But let it be something that's not very long.'
    With a roly poly, gammon and spinach,
    Heigho, says Anthony Rowley!

'Indeed, Mrs Mouse,' replied the frog,
    Heigho, says Rowley,
'A cold has made me as hoarse as a dog.'
    With a roly poly, gammon and spinach,
    Heigho, says Anthony Rowley!

'Since you have caught cold, Mr Frog,' Mousey said,
  Heigho, says Rowley,
'I'll sing you a song that I have just made.'
  With a roly poly, gammon and spinach,
  Heigho, says Anthony Rowley!

But while they were all merry-making,
  Heigho, says Rowley,
A cat and her kittens came tumbling in.
  With a roly poly, gammon and spinach,
  Heigho, says Anthony Rowley!

The cat she seized the rat by the crown;
  Heigho, says Rowley,
The kittens they pulled the little mouse down.
  With a roly poly, gammon and spinach,
  Heigho, says Anthony Rowley!

This put Mr Frog in a terrible fright,
  Heigho, says Rowley,
He took up his hat and he wished them good night.
  With a roly poly, gammon and spinach,
  Heigho, says Anthony Rowley!

But as Froggy was crossing over a brook,
  Heigho, says Rowley,
A lily-white duck came and gobbled him up.
  With a roly poly, gammon and spinach,
  Heigho, says Anthony Rowley!

So there was an end of one, two, and three,
  Heigho, says Rowley,
The rat, the mouse, and the little frog-gy!
  With a roly poly, gammon and spinach,
  Heigho, says Anthony Rowley!

THERE WAS A MAN OF NEWINGTON

There was a man of Newington,
　　And he was wondrous wise,
He jumped into a quickset hedge,
　　And scratched out both his eyes:
But when he saw his eyes were out,
　　With all his might and main
He jumped into another hedge,
　　And scratched them in again.

52

PAT-A-CAKE, PAT-A-CAKE, BAKER'S MAN!

Pat-a-cake, pat-a-cake, baker's man!
  Make me a cake as fast as I can;
Pat it, and prick it, and mark it with 'T',
  Put it in the oven for Tommy and me.

HANDY ANDY

Handy Andy, Jack-a-dandy,
Loved plum-cake and sugar candy;
He bought some at a grocer's shop,
And out he came, hop, hop, hop, hop.

THE GRAND OLD DUKE OF YORK

O, the Grand Old Duke of York,
  He had ten thousand men;
He marched them up to the top of the hill,
  Then marched them down again!
O, and when they were up, they were up,
  And when they were down, they were down;
And when they were only halfway up,
  They were neither up nor down.

OLD MOTHER HUBBARD

Old Mother Hubbard
Went to the cupboard
To get her poor dog a bone;
But when she got there
The cupboard was bare,
And so the poor dog had none.

She went to the baker's
To buy him some bread;
But when she came back
The poor dog was dead.

She went to the joiner's
To buy him a coffin;
But when she came back
The poor dog was laughing.

She took a clean dish
To get him some tripe;
But when she came back
He was smoking a pipe.

She went to the ale-house
To buy him some beer;
But when she came back
The dog sat in a chair.

She went to the tavern
For white wine and red;
But when she came back
The dog stood on his head.

She went to the hatter's
To buy him a hat;
But when she came back
He was feeding the cat.

She went to the barber's
To buy him a wig;
But when she came back
He was dancing a jig.

She went to the fruiterer's
To buy him some fruit;
But when she came back
He was playing the flute.

She went to the tailor's
To buy him a coat;
But when she came back
He was riding a goat.

She went to the cobbler's
To buy him some shoes;
But when she came back
He was reading the news.

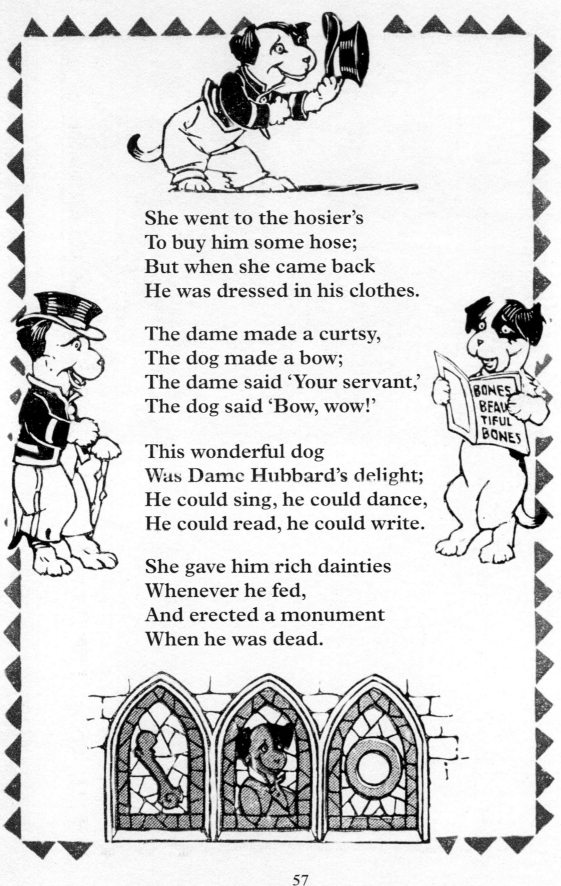

She went to the hosier's
To buy him some hose;
But when she came back
He was dressed in his clothes.

The dame made a curtsy,
The dog made a bow;
The dame said 'Your servant,'
The dog said 'Bow, wow!'

This wonderful dog
Was Dame Hubbard's delight;
He could sing, he could dance,
He could read, he could write.

She gave him rich dainties
Whenever he fed,
And erected a monument
When he was dead.

There Was An Old Woman Who Lived In A Shoe

There was an old woman who lived in a shoe,
She had so many children she didn't know what
    to do;
She gave them some broth without any bread;
She whipped them all soundly and put them to bed.

To Bed, To Bed

'To bed, to bed,'
  Says Sleepy-head;
'Tarry awhile,' says Slow;
  'Put on the pan,'
Says hungry Nan,
  'Let's sup before we go.'

DEEDLE, DEEDLE, DUMPLING

Deedle, deedle, dumpling, my son John,
He went to bed with his stockings on;
One shoe off, and one shoe on,
Deedle, deedle, dumpling, my son John.

COCK-A-DOODLE-DOO

Cock-a-doodle-doo!
My dame has lost her shoe;
My master's lost his fiddle-stick,
And doesn't know what to do.

Cock-a-doodle-doo!
My dame has found her shoe,
And master's found his fiddle-stick,
Cock-a-doodle-doo!

Cock-a-doodle-doo!
My dame shall dance with you,
My master's found his fiddle-stick,
Cock-a-doodle-doo!

MOLLY AND I

Molly, my sister, and I fell out,
And what do you think it was about?
She loved coffee, and I loved tea,
And that was the reason we couldn't agree.

JACK SPRAT

Jack Sprat could eat no fat,
   His wife could eat no lean,
And so between them both, you see,
   They licked the platter clean.
Jack ate all the lean,
   His wife ate all the fat,
The bone they picked it clean,
   Then gave it to the cat.

I HAD A LITTLE NUT-TREE

I had a little nut-tree, nothing would it bear
But a silver nutmeg and a golden pear;
The King of Spain's daughter came to visit me,
And all because of my little nut-tree.
I skipped over water, I danced over sea,
And all the birds in the air couldn't catch me.

PEASE PUDDING HOT

Pease pudding hot,
  Pease pudding cold,
Pease pudding in the pot,
  Nine days old.

Some like it hot,
  Some like it cold,
Some like it in the pot,
  Nine days old.

A CAT CAME FIDDLING OUT OF A BARN

A cat came fiddling out of a barn,
With a pair of bagpipes under her arm;
She could sing nothing but fiddle-de-dee,
The mouse has married the bumblebee;
Pipe, cat – dance, mouse –
We'll have a wedding at our good house.

SIMPLE SIMON

Simple Simon met a pieman
   Going to the fair;
Says Simple Simon to the pieman,
   'Let me taste your ware.'

      Says the pieman to Simple Simon,
         'Show me first your penny';
      Says Simple Simon to the pieman,
         'Indeed I have not any.'

Simple Simon went a-fishing
   For to catch a whale;
All the water he had got
   Was in his mother's pail.

      Simple Simon went to look
         If plums grew on a thistle;
      He pricked his fingers very much,
         Which made poor Simon whistle.

MONDAY

TUESDAY

SOLOMON GRUNDY

SOLOMON GRUNDY

Solomon Grundy,
Born on a Monday,
Christened on Tuesday,
Married on Wednesday,
Took ill on Thursday,
Worse on Friday,
Died on Saturday,
Buried on Sunday.
This is the end
Of Solomon Grundy.

WEDNESDAY

THURSDAY

FRIDAY   **SATURDAY**   **SUNDAY**

HERE LIES — SOLOMON GRUNDY = SEVEN DAYS MAKE ONE WEAK

LITTLE MISS MUFFET

Little Miss Muffet
  Sat on a tuffet,
    Eating her curds and whey;
     There came a big spider,
      Who sat down beside her,
       And frightened Miss Muffet away.

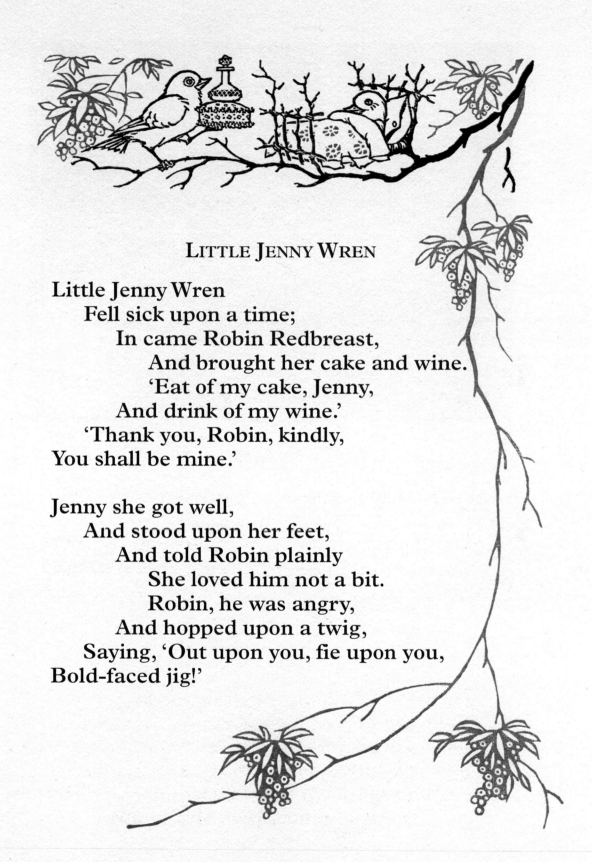

LITTLE JENNY WREN

Little Jenny Wren
　　Fell sick upon a time;
　　　　In came Robin Redbreast,
　　　　　　And brought her cake and wine.
　　　　　'Eat of my cake, Jenny,
　　　　And drink of my wine.'
　　'Thank you, Robin, kindly,
You shall be mine.'

Jenny she got well,
　　And stood upon her feet,
　　　　And told Robin plainly
　　　　　　She loved him not a bit.
　　　　　Robin, he was angry,
　　　　And hopped upon a twig,
　　Saying, 'Out upon you, fie upon you,
Bold-faced jig!'

WEE WILLIE WINKLE

Wee Willie Winkle runs through the town,
Upstairs and downstairs in his nightgown,
Rapping at the window, crying through the lock,
'Are the children in their beds, for now it's eight
    o'clock?'

FOR WANT OF A NAIL, THE SHOE WAS LOST

For want of a nail, the shoe was lost,
For want of the shoe, the horse was lost,
For want of the horse, the rider was lost,
For want of the rider, the battle was lost,
For want of the battle, the kingdom was lost,
And all for want of a horseshoe nail!

TEN LITTLE MICE

Ten little mice sat down to spin,
Pussy passed by, and puss looked in:
'What are you at, my jolly ten?'
'We're making coats for gentlemen.'
'Shall I come in and cut your threads?'
'No, Mister Puss, you'd bite off our heads.'

COCK ROBIN GOT UP EARLY

Cock Robin got up early
    At the break of day,
And went to Jenny's window
    To sing a roundelay.

He sang Cock Robin's love
    To the little Jenny Wren,
And when he got unto the end,
    Then he began again.

PETER PIPER

Peter Piper picked a peck of pickled pepper;
A peck of pickled pepper Peter Piper picked;
If Peter Piper picked a peck of pickled pepper,
Where's the peck of pickled pepper Peter Piper
    picked?

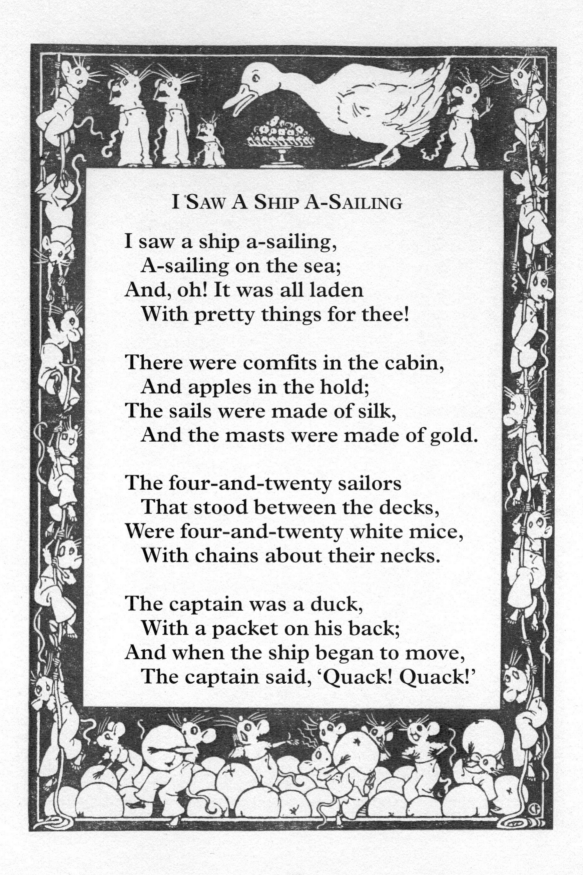

I Saw A Ship A-Sailing

I saw a ship a-sailing,
   A-sailing on the sea;
And, oh! It was all laden
   With pretty things for thee!

There were comfits in the cabin,
   And apples in the hold;
The sails were made of silk,
   And the masts were made of gold.

The four-and-twenty sailors
   That stood between the decks,
Were four-and-twenty white mice,
   With chains about their necks.

The captain was a duck,
   With a packet on his back;
And when the ship began to move,
   The captain said, 'Quack! Quack!'

I·SAW·A·SHIP·A-SAILING·A-SAILING·ON·THE·SEA;
·AND·OH!·IT·WAS·ALL·LADEN·WITH·PRETTY·THINGS·FOR·THEE!

Baa, Baa, Black Sheep

'Baa, baa, black sheep, have you any wool?'
'Yes, sir; yes, sir, three bags full:
One for my master, one for my dame,
And one for the little boy that lives down the lane.'

When I Was A Little Boy

When I was a little boy
   I had but little wit;
It is some time ago,
   And I've no more yet.

Nor ever, ever shall
   Until I die,
For the longer I live
   The more fool am I.

Doctor Foster Went To Gloucester

Doctor Foster went to Gloucester,
   In a shower of rain,
He stepped in a puddle, up to the middle,
   And never went there again.

Old Mother Goose!
When she wanted to wander,
Would ride though the air
On a very fine gander.

Mother Goose had a house,
'Twas built in a wood,
An owl at the door
For a porter stood.

She had a son Jack,
A plain-looking lad,
He was not very good,
Nor yet very bad.

She sent him to market,
A live goose he bought:
'Here! Mother,' says he,
'It will not go for naught.'

Jack's goose and her gander
Grew very fond;
They'd both eat together,
Or swim in one pond.

Jack found one morning,
As I have been told,
His goose had laid him
An egg of pure gold.

Jack rode to his mother,
The news for to tell.
She called him a good boy,
And said it was well.

THE MAN IN THE MOON

The man in the moon
Came tumbling down,
And asked the way to Norwich;
He went by south,
And burnt his mouth
Eating cold pease porridge.

LONDON BRIDGE IS FALLING DOWN

London Bridge is falling down,
Falling down, falling down
London Bridge is falling down,
My fair lady.

We must build it up again,
Up again, up again
We must build it up again,
My fair lady.

THERE WAS A CROOKED MAN

There was a crooked man, and he went a crooked
mile,
He found a crooked sixpence against a crooked stile:
He bought a crooked cat which caught a crooked
mouse,
And they all lived together in a little crooked house.

POP GOES THE WEASEL

Half a pound o' tupenny rice,
Half a pound o' treacle;
That's the way the money goes,
Pop goes the weasel!

THREE BLIND MICE

Three blind mice, three blind mice
  See how they run! See how they run!
They all ran after the farmer's wife,
  Who cut off their tails with a carving-knife;
Did you ever see such a thing in your life
  As three blind mice?

HOT-CROSS BUNS

Hot-cross buns!
Hot-cross buns!
One a penny, two a penny,
Hot-cross buns!

If you have no daughters
Give them to your sons.
One a penny, two a penny,
Hot-cross buns!

ORANGES AND LEMONS

'Oranges and lemons', say the bells of St Clements.
'You owe me five farthings', say the bells of
    St Martin's.
'When will you pay me?' say the bells of Old
    Bailey.
'When I grow rich', say the bells of Shoreditch.
'When will that be?' say the bells of Stepney.
'I do not know', says the great bell of Bow.

Here comes a candle to light you to bed!
Here comes a chopper to chop off your head!

'Pancakes and fritters', say the bells of St Peter's.
'Two sticks and an apple', say the bells of
    Whitechapel.
'Old Father Baldpate', say the slow bells at
    Aldgate.
'Poker and tongs', say the bells at St John's.
'Kettles and pans', say the bells of St Ann's.
'Brick-bats and tiles', say the bells of St Giles.

Here comes a candle to light you to bed!
Here comes a chopper to chop off your head!

HERE WE GO ROUND THE MULBERRY BUSH

Here we go round the mulberry bush,
  Mulberry bush, mulberry bush,
Here we go round the mulberry bush,
  On a cold and frosty morning.

This is the way we wash our hands,
  Wash our hands, wash our hands,
This is the way we wash our hands,
  On a cold and frosty morning.

This is the way we dry our hands,
  Dry our hands, dry our hands,
This is the way we dry our hands,
  On a cold and frosty morning.

This is the way we clap our hands,
  Clap our hands, clap our hands,
This is the way we clap our hands,
  On a cold and frosty morning.

This is the way we warm our hands,
  Warm our hands, warm our hands,
This is the way we warm our hands,
  On a cold and frosty morning.

MARCH WINDS AND APRIL SHOWERS

March winds and April showers
Bring forth May flowers.

SLEEP, BABY, SLEEP

Sleep, baby, sleep.
Our valley home is deep.
The little lamb is on the green,
With snowy fleece, so soft and clean.
Sleep, baby, sleep.

HICKORY, DICKORY, DOCK

Hickory, dickory, dock!
The mouse ran up the clock.
The clock struck one,
        The mouse ran down,
Hickory, dickory, dock!

WHISTLE, DAUGHTER, WHISTLE

'Whistle, daughter, whistle,
    Whistle, daughter dear.'
'I cannot whistle, mammy,
    I cannot whistle clear.'
'Whistle, daughter, whistle,
    Whistle for a groat.'
'I cannot whistle, mammy,
    I cannot make a note.'

A RING O' ROSES

A ring, a ring o' roses,
    A pocketful of posies,
Atishoo! Atishoo!
    We all fall down.

THE TWO LITTLE KITTENS

Two little kittens, one stormy night,
Began to quarrel, and then to fight.

'I'll have that mouse,' said the bigger cat.
'You'll have that mouse? We'll see about that!'

'I WILL have that mouse,' said the older one.
'You SHAN'T have the mouse,' said the little one.

I told you before 'twas a stormy night,
When these two little kittens began to fight.

The old woman seized her sweeping-broom,
And swept the two kittens right out of the room.

The ground was all covered with frost and snow,
And the two little kittens had nowhere to go.

So they lay them down on the mat at the door,
While the old woman finished sweeping the floor.

Then they crept in as quiet as mice,
All wet with the snow, and as cold as ice.

For they found it much better, that stormy night,
To lie down and sleep, than to quarrel and fight.

OH WHERE, OH WHERE IS MY LITTLE DOG GONE?

Oh where, oh where is my little dog gone?
　Oh where, oh where can he be?
His hair was short but his tail was long,
　Oh where, oh where can he be?

TIGGY TOUCHWOOD

Tiggy-tiggy-touchwood, my black hen,
She lays eggs for gentlemen,
Sometimes nine and sometimes ten,
Tiggy-tiggy-touchwood, my black hen.

LITTLE CLOTHILDA

Little Clothilda,
　Well and hearty,
Thought she'd like
　To give a party.

But as her friends
　Were shy and wary,
Nobody came
　But her own canary.

CHRISTMAS COMES

Christmas comes but once a year,
And when it comes it brings good cheer.

LITTLE JACK HORNER

Little Jack Horner
Sat in a corner,
Eating a Christmas pie;
He put in his thumb,
And pulled out a plum,
And said: 'What a good boy am I!'

I LOVE LITTLE PUSSY

I love little pussy, her coat is so warm,
And if I don't hurt her, she'll do me no harm;
I'll not pull her tail, nor drive her away,
But pussy and I together will play.

OH·DEAR·WHAT·CAN·THE·MATTER·BE

Oh dear, what can the matter be?
  Dear, dear, what can the matter be?
Oh, dear, what can the matter be?
  Johnny's so long at the fair.

He promised to buy me a trinket to please me,
  And then for a kiss – oh, he vowed he would
    tease me!
He promised to buy me a bunch of blue ribbons
  To tie up my bonny brown hair.

He promised to buy me a basket of posies,
  A garland of lilies, a garland of roses,
A little straw hat to set off the blue ribbons,
  That tie up my bonny brown hair!

Oh dear, what can the matter be?
  Dear, dear, what can the matter be?
Oh dear, what can the matter be?
  Johnny's so long at the fair.

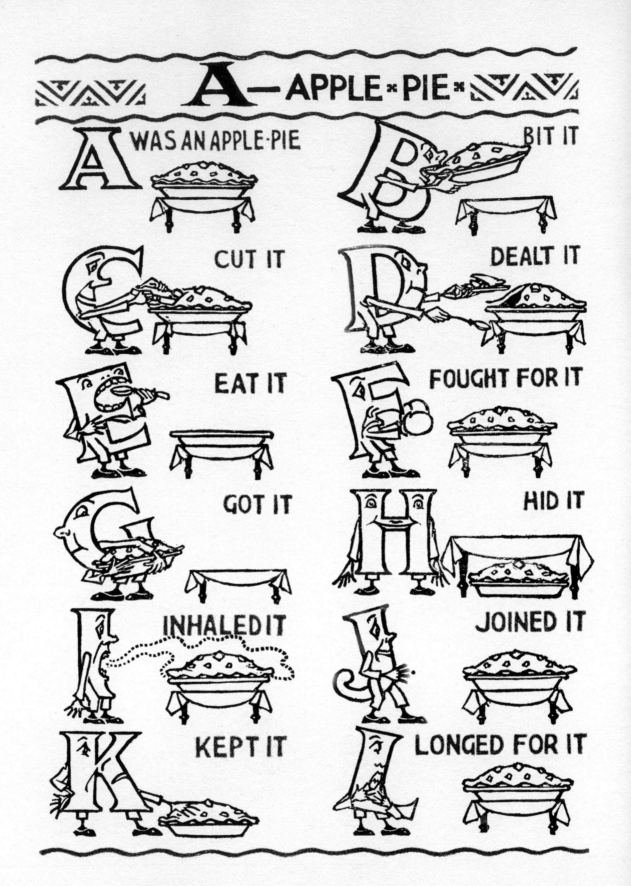

A — APPLE·PIE

A WAS AN APPLE·PIE

B BIT IT

C CUT IT

D DEALT IT

E EAT IT

F FOUGHT FOR IT

G GOT IT

H HID IT

I INHALED IT

J JOINED IT

K KEPT IT

L LONGED FOR IT

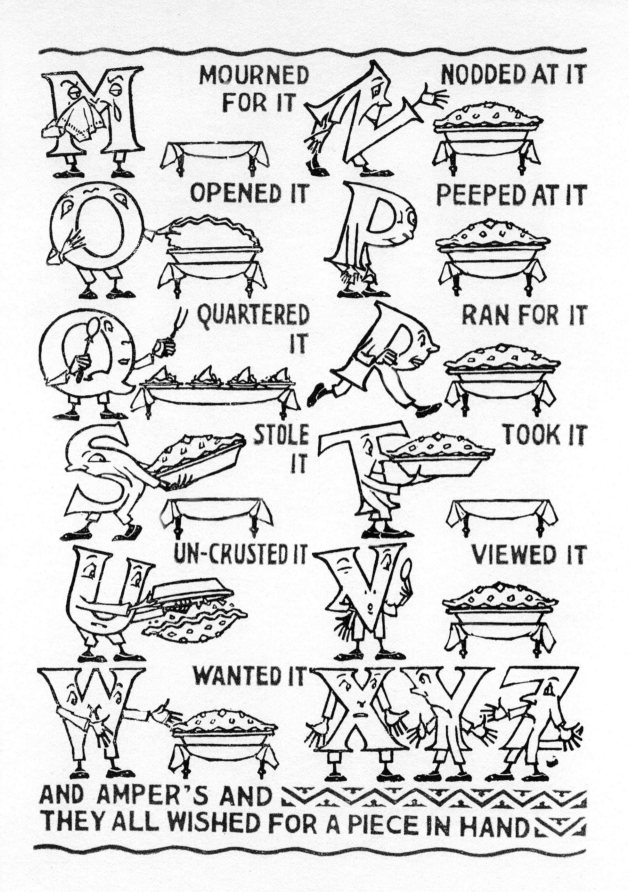

MOURNED FOR IT

NODDED AT IT

OPENED IT

PEEPED AT IT

QUARTERED IT

RAN FOR IT

STOLE IT

TOOK IT

UN-CRUSTED IT

VIEWED IT

WANTED IT

AND AMPER'S AND
THEY ALL WISHED FOR A PIECE IN HAND

JACK AND JILL

Jack and Jill went up the hill
    To fetch a pail of water;
Jack fell down and broke his crown
    And Jill came tumbling after.

Up Jack got, and home did trot
    As fast as he could caper,
Went to bed to mend his head
    With vinegar and brown paper.

ONE, TWO, THREE, FOUR, FIVE

One, two, three, four, five,
Once I caught a fish alive,
Six, seven, eight, nine, ten,
Then I let him go again.
Why did you let him go?
Because he bit my finger so!
Which finger did he bite?
This little finger on the right!

IF ALL THE WORLD WERE PAPER

If all the world were paper,
And all the sea were ink;
And all the trees were bread and cheese,
What would we do for drink?

PETER, PETER, PUMPKIN-EATER

Peter, Peter, pumpkin-eater,
Had a wife and couldn't keep her;
He put her in a pumpkin shell,
And there he kept her very well.

TO MARKET, TO MARKET

To market, to market, to buy a fat pig,
Home again, home again, jiggety jig.
To market, to market, to buy a fat hog,
Home again, home again, joggety jog.

RIDE A COCK-HORSE

Ride a cock-horse to Banbury Cross,
   To see a fine lady ride on a white horse!
Rings on her fingers and bells on her toes,
   She shall have music wherever she goes.

HEY, DIDDLE DIDDLE

Hey, diddle diddle, the cat and the fiddle,
The cow jumped over the moon;
The little dog laughed to see such sport,
And the dish ran away with the spoon!

LUCY LOCKET

Lucy Locket lost her pocket,
  Kitty Fisher found it,
But ne'er a penny was there in it
  Except the binding round it.

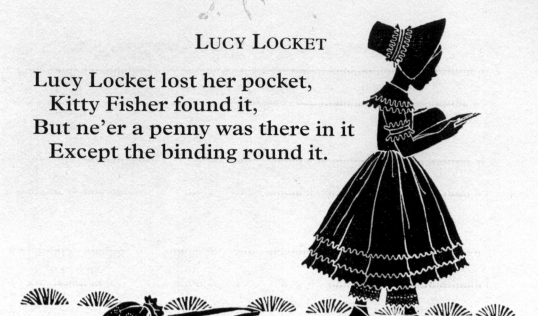

FE, FI, FO, FUM

Fe, fi, fo, fum
I smell the blood of an Englishman!
Be he alive or be he dead,
I'll grind his bones to make my bread!

DAFFY-DOWN-DILLY

Daffy-down-dilly has come up to town,
In a yellow petticoat and a green gown.

PLEASE TO REMEMBER THE FIFTH OF NOVEMBER

Please to remember the fifth of November,
  Gunpowder, treason, and plot,
I see no reason why gunpowder treason
  Should ever be forgot.

HUSH-A-BYE, BABY

Hush-a-bye, baby, on the tree top,
When the wind blows the cradle will rock;
When the bough bends the cradle will fall,
Down will come baby, bough, cradle and all.

IF ALL THE SEA WERE ONE SEA

If all the sea were one sea,
What a great sea that would be!
And if all the trees were one tree,
What a great tree that would be!

And if all the axes were one axe,
What a great axe that would be!
And if all the men were one man,
What a great man that would be!

And if the great man took the great axe
And cut down the great tree
And let it fall into the sea,
What a splish splash that would be!

FROGGY BOGGY

Froggy boggy
  Tried to jump
On a stone,
  And got a bump.

It made his eyes
  Wink and frown,
And turned his nose
  Upside down.

GOOSEY, GOOSEY, GANDER

Goosey, goosey, gander,
  Whither shall I wander
Upstairs, and downstairs,
  And in my lady's chamber.
There I met an old man,
  Who would not say his prayers,
I took him by his left leg
  And threw him down the stairs.

A WEEK OF BIRTHDAYS

Monday's child is fair of face,
Tuesday's child is full of grace,
Wednesday's child is full of woe,
Thursday's child has far to go,
Friday's child is loving and giving,
Saturday's child works hard for its living,
But the child that is born on the Sabbath day
Is wise and wonderful, blithe and gay.

BESSIE BELL AND MARY GRAY

Bessie Bell and Mary Gray,
   They were two bonnie lasses:
They built their house upon the lea,
   And covered it with rushes.

Bessie kept the garden gate,
   And Mary kept the pantry;
Bessie always had to wait,
   While Mary lived in plenty.

I HAD A LITTLE HOBBY-HORSE

I had a little hobby-horse,
And it was dapple grey;
Its head was made of pea-straw,
Its tail was made of hay.

I sold it to an old woman
For a copper groat;
And I'll not sing my song again
Without a brand new coat.

BREAKFAST....DINNER........TEA........SUPPER

THERE WAS AN OLD WOMAN OF NORWICH

There was an old woman of Norwich,
Who lived upon nothing but porridge;
Parading the town,
She turned cloak into gown,
This thrifty old woman of Norwich.

BUZ, QUOTH THE BLUE-FLY

Buz, quoth the blue-fly,
Hum, quoth the bee,
Buz and hum they cry,
And so do we.

In his ear, in his nose
Thus, do you see?
He ate the dormouse,
Sure, it was he.

THREE YOUNG RATS

Three young rats with black felt hats,
Three young ducks with white straw flats,
Three young dogs with curling tails,
Three young cats with demi-veils,
Went out to walk with two young pigs
In satin vests and sorrel wigs;
But suddenly it chanced to rain,
And so they all went home again.

RUB-A-DUB-DUB

Rub-a-dub-dub,
Three men in a tub,
And what do you think they be?
The butcher, thc baker,
The candlestick maker,
They all sailed out to sea.

WHAT DO I SEE?

What do I see?
  A bumble-bee
Sit on a rose
  And wink at me!

What do you mean
  By hum, hum, hum?
If you mean me,
  I dare not come!

95

LITTLE DOG, LITTLE DOG

Little dog, little dog,
  What do you there?

                Curly my tail, lady,
                  Under the chair.

Little dog, little dog,
  Hear you what's said?

                Often and often,
                  My dear little maid.

Little dog, little dog,
  Think you men wise?

                In closing their ears
                  And shutting their eyes.

DIRTY JACK

There was one little Jack, not very long back,
And 'tis told to his lasting disgrace,
That he never was seen with his hands at all clean,
Nor yet ever clean was his face.

When to wash he was sent, he sulkily went,
With water to splash himself o'er:
But he left the black streaks all over his cheeks,
And made them look worse than before.

His friends were much hurt to see so much dirt,
And often and well did they scour;
But all was in vain, he was dirty again,
Before they had done it an hour.

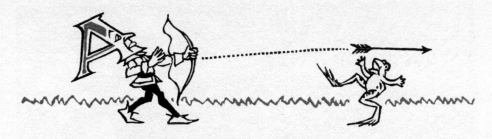

A WAS AN ARCHER

A was an Archer, who shot at a frog.
B was a Butcher, who had a great dog.
C was a Captain, all covered with lace.
D was a Dunce, with a very sad face.
E was an Esquire, with pride on his brow.
F was a Farmer, who followed the plough.
G was a Gamester, who had but ill luck.
H was a Hunter, who hunted a buck.
I was an Innkeeper, who loved to carouse.
J was a Joiner, who built up a house.
K was a King, so mighty and grand.
L was a Lady, who had a white hand.
M was a Miser, who hoarded his gold.
N was a Noblemen, gallant and bold.
O was an Oysterman, who went about town.
P was a Parson, who wore a black gown.
Q was a Quack, with a wonderful pill.
R was a Robber, who wanted to kill.
S was a Sailor, who spent all he got.
T was a Tinker, who mended a pot.
U was a Usurer, a miserable elf.
V was a Vintner, who drank all himself.
W was a Watchman, who guarded the door.
X was Expensive, and so became poor.
Y was a Youth, that did not love school.
Z was a Zany, a poor harmless fool.

The Fairy Queen

A little fairy comes at night,
Her eyes are blue, her hair is brown,
With silver spots upon her wing,
As from the moon she flutters down.

She has a little silver wand,
And when a good child goes to bed,
She waves her wand from right to left,
And makes a circle round its head.

And then it dreams of pleasant things,
Of fountains filled with fairy fish,
And trees that bear delicious fruit,
And bow their branches at a wish.

And talking birds, with gifted tongues,
For singing songs, and telling tales;
And pretty dwarfs to show the way
Through fairy hills and fairy dales.

But when the bad child goes to bed,
From left to right she waves her wings,
And then it dreams all through the night
Of only ugly, horrid things.

Then naughty children wake and weep,
And wish the long black gloom away;
But good ones love the dark, and find
The night as pleasant as the day.

SING A SONG O' SIXPENCE

Sing a song o' sixpence,
   A pocket full of rye;
Four-and-twenty blackbirds
   Baked in a pie.
When the pie was opened
   The birds began to sing,
Was not that a dainty dish
   To set before the King?

The King was in his counting-house
   Counting out his money;
The Queen was in the parlour
   Eating bread and honey;
The maid was in the garden
   Hanging out the clothes,
When down came a blackbird
   And pecked off her nose.

FAERY SONG

Shed no tear! Oh shed no tear!
The flower will bloom another year.
Weep no more! Oh weep no more!
Young buds sleep in the root's white core.
Dry your eyes; oh dry your eyes!
For I was taught in paradise
To ease my breast of melodies –
       Shed no tear.

Overhead! Look overhead!
Among the blossoms white and red –
Shed no tear! Oh shed no tear!
The flower will bloom another year.

A LANE

From house to house he goes,
   A messenger small and slight;
And whether it rains or snows,
   He sleeps outside in the night.

A KING AND HIS DAUGHTERS

There was a King, and he had three daughters,
And they all lived in a basin of water;
    The basin bended,
    And my story's ended.
If the basin had been stronger
My story would have been longer.

ROBIN HOOD

Robin Hood, Robin Hood,
Is in the mickle wood!
Little John, Little John,
He to the town is gone.
Robin Hood, Robin Hood,
    Is telling his beads,
All in the greenwood,
    Among the green weeds.
Little John, Little John,
    If he comes no more,
Robin Hood, Robin Hood,
    We shall fret full sore!

HOW DOTH THE LITTLE BUSY BEE

How doth the little busy bee
    Improve each shining hour,
And gather honey day by day
    From every opening flower!

THE NORTH WIND DOTH BLOW

The north wind doth blow,
And we shall have snow,
And what will poor Robin do then, poor thing?

He'll sit in a barn,
And keep himself warm,
And hide his head under his wing, poor thing.

ROBIN HOOD

THE SPIDER AND THE FLY

'Will you walk into my parlour?'
    Said the spider to the fly;
    ''Tis the prettiest little parlour
    That ever you did spy.
The way into my parlour
    Is up a winding stair;
And I have many curious things
    To show you when you're there.'
'Oh, no, no,' said the little fly;
    'To ask me is in vain;
For who goes up your winding stair
    Can ne'er come down again.'

'I'm sure you must be weary, dear,
    With soaring up so high;
Will you rest upon my little bed?'
    Said the Spider to the fly.
'There are pretty curtains drawn around;
    The sheets are fine and thin;

And if you like to rest awhile,
    I'll snugly tuck you in!'
'Oh, no, no,' said the little fly;
    'For I've often heard it said,
They never, never wake again
    Who sleep upon your bed.'

Said the cunning spider to the fly, –
    'Dear friend, what can I do
To prove the warm affection
    I've always felt for you?'
'I thank you, gentle sir,' she said,
    'For what you're pleased to say,
And bidding you good morning now,
    I'll call another day.'

The spider turned him round about,
    And went into his den,
For well he knew the silly fly
    Would soon come back again;
So he wove a subtle web
    In a little corner sly,
And set his table ready
    To dine upon the fly.
Then he came out to his door again,
    And merrily did he sing, –
'Come hither, hither, pretty fly,
    With the pearl and silver wing;
Your robes are green and purple,
    There's a crest upon your head!
Your eyes are like the diamond bright,
    But mine are dull as lead!'

Alas! Alas! How very soon
    This silly little fly,
Hearing his wily, flattering words,
    Came slowly flitting by.
With buzzing wings she hung aloft,
    Then near and nearer drew,
Thinking only of her brilliant eyes,
    Her green and purple hue, –
Thinking only of her crested head, –
    Poor foolish thing! At last,
Up jumped the cunning spider,
    And fiercely held her fast!
He dragged her up his winding stair,
    Into his dismal den,
Within his parlour, –
    But she ne'er came out again!

And now, dear little children,
    Who may this story read,
To idle, silly flattering words,
    I pray you ne'er give heed;
Unto an evil counsellor
    Close heart and ear and eye,
And take a lesson from this tale
    Of the Spider and the Fly.

THE CAT AND THE MOUSE

The cat and the mouse
Played in the malt-house:

The cat bit the mouse's tail off. 'Pray, puss, give me my tail.' 'No,' said the cat, 'I'll not give you your tail till you go to the cow and fetch me some milk.'

First she leapt, and then she ran,
Till she came to the cow, and so began:

'Pray, cow, give me milk, that I may give cat milk, that cat may give me my own tail again.' 'No,' said the cow, 'I will give you no milk, till you go to the farmer and get me some hay.'

First she leapt, and then she ran,
Till she came to the farmer, and so began:

'Pray, farmer, give me hay, that I may give cow hay, that cow may give me milk, that I may give cat milk, that cat may give me my own tail again.' 'No,' says the farmer, 'I'll give you no hay, till you go to the butcher and fetch me some meat.'

First she leapt, and then she ran,
Till she came to the butcher, and so began:

'Pray, butcher, give me meat, that I may give farmer meat, that farmer may give me hay, that I may give cow hay, that cow may give me milk, that I may give cat milk, that cat may give me my own tail again.' 'No,' says the butcher, 'I'll give you no meat, till you go to the baker and fetch me some bread.'

First she leapt, and then she ran,
Till she came to the baker, and so began:

'Pray, baker, give me bread, that I may give
butcher bread, that butcher may give me
meat, that I may give farmer meat, that
farmer may give me hay, that I may give cow
hay, that cow may give me milk, that I may
give cat milk, that cat may give me my own
tail again.'

'Yes,' said the baker, 'I'll give you some bread,
But if you eat my grain, I'll cut off your head.'

Then the baker gave mouse bread, and
mouse gave butcher bread, and butcher gave
mouse meat, and mouse gave farmer meat,
and farmer gave mouse hay, and mouse gave
cow hay, and cow gave mouse milk, and
mouse gave cat milk, and cat gave mouse her
own tail again!

And so she leapt, and so she ran,
For the mouse had her own tail again!

Mr Nobody

I know a funny little man, as quiet as a mouse,
Who does the mischief that is done in everybody's
    house:
There's no one ever sees his face – and yet we all
    agree
That every plate we break was cracked by
    Mr Nobody.

'Tis he who always tears our books and leaves the
    door ajar;
He pulls the buttons off our shirts, and scatters pins
    afar;
That squeaky door will always squeak, for prithee,
    don't you see,
We leave the oiling to be done by Mr Nobody.

He puts damp wood upon the fire, that kettles
    cannot boil;
His are the feet that bring in mud, and all the
    carpets soil:
The papers always are mislaid – who had been last
    but he?
There's no one tosses things about but
    Mr Nobody!

The finger-marks upon the door by none of *us* are
    made;
We never leave the blinds unclosed to let the
    curtains fade:
The ink *we* never spill; the boots, that lying round
    we see,
Are not *our* boots: they all belong to Mr Nobody!

Will You Walk A Little Faster?

'Will you walk a little faster?' said a whiting to a
    snail,
'There's a porpoise close behind us, and he's treading
    on my tail.
See how eagerly the lobsters and the turtles all
    advance!
They are waiting on the shingle – will you come and
    join the dance?
Will you, won't you, will you, won't you, will you
    join the dance?'

'What matters it how far we go?' his scaly friend
    replied.
'There is another shore, you know, upon the other side.
The farther off from England, the nearer is to France –
Then turn not pale, beloved snail, but come and
    join the dance.
Will you, won't you, will you, won't you, will you
    join the dance?'

'You can really have no notion how delightful it will be,
When they take us up and throw us, with the lobsters,
    out to sea!'
But the snail replied, 'Too far, too far!' and gave a look
    askance –

Said he thanked the whiting kindly, but he would not
    join that dance.
Would not, could not, would not, could not, would not
    join the dance.
Would not, could not, would not, could not, would not
    join the dance.

THE MARRIAGE OF COCK ROBIN AND JENNY WREN

It was on a merry time
　　When Jenny Wren was young,
So neatly as she danced,
　　And so sweetly as she sung.

Robin Redbreast lost his heart,
　　He was a gallant bird;
He doffed his hat to Jenny
　　And thus to her he said:

'My dearest Jenny Wren,
　　If you will be but mine,
You shall dine on cherry pie,
　　And drink nice currant wine;

'I'll dress you like a goldfinch,
　　Or like a peacock gay;
So if you'll have me, Jenny,
　　Let us appoint the day.'

Jenny blushed behind her fan,
　　And thus declared her mind:
'Then let it be tomorrow, Bob,
　　I take your offer kind;

'Cherry pie is very good,
  So is currant wine;
But I'll wear my russet gown,
  And never dress too fine.'

Robin rose up early
  At the break of day,
He flew to Jenny Wren's house,
  To sing a roundelay.

He sang of Robin's love
  For little Jenny Wren,
And when he came unto the end,
  Then he began again.

The birds were asked to dine;
  Not Jenny's friends alone,
But every pretty songster
  That had Cock Robin known.

They had a cherry pie,
  Besides some currant wine;
And every guest bought something,
  That sumptuous they might dine.

Wynken, Blynken, and Nod

Wynken, Blynken, and Nod one night,
　Sailed off in a wooden shoe,
Sailed on a river of misty light,
　Into a sea of dew.
'Where are you going, and what do you wish?'
　The old moon asked the three;
'We have come to fish for the herring-fish
　That live in this beautiful sea;
Nets and silver and gold have we';
　Said Wynken, Blynken, and Nod.

The old moon laughed and sang a song
　As they rocked in the wooden shoe;
The wind that sped them all night long
　Ruffled the waves of dew.
The little stars were the herring-fish
　That lived in the beautiful sea.
'Now cast your nets wherever you wish,
　But never afraid are we';
So cried the stars to the fishermen three,
　Wynken, Blynken, and Nod.

All night long their nets they threw
　For the fish in the twinkling foam,
Then down from the sky came the wooden shoe,
　Bringing the fisherman home.
'Twas all so pretty a sail, it seemed
　As if it could not be,
And some folk thought 'twas a dream they
　　dreamed
Of sailing that beautiful sea.

But I shall name you fishermen three,
  Wynken, Blynken, and Nod.

Wynken and Blynken are two little eyes,
  And Nod is a little head,
And the wooden shoe that sailed the skies,
  Is a wee one's trundle-bed.
So shut your eyes while mother sings
  Of wonderful sights that be,
And you shall see the beautiful things
  As you rock on the misty sea,
Where the old shoe rocked the fishermen three,
  Wynken, Blynken, and Nod.

TOPSY TURVY

If the butterfly courted the bee,
And the owl the porcupine;
If churches were built in the sea,
And three times one was nine;
If the pony rode his master,
If the buttercups ate the cows,
If the cat had the dire disaster
To be worried, sir, by the mouse;
If mamma, sir, sold the baby
To a lady for half a crown;
If a gentleman, sir, was a lady,
The world would be Upside-Down!
If any or all of these wonders
Should ever come about,
I should not consider them blunders,
For I should be Inside-Out!

THERE WAS AN OLD MAN WITH A BEARD

There was an old man with a beard,
Who said, 'It is just as I fear'd! –
   Two Owls and a Hen,
   Four Larks and a Wren,
Have all built their nests in my beard!'

BAT, BAT

Bat, bat, come under my hat,
   And I'll give you a slice of bacon,
And when I bake I'll give you a cake,
   If I am not mistaken.

THE
END

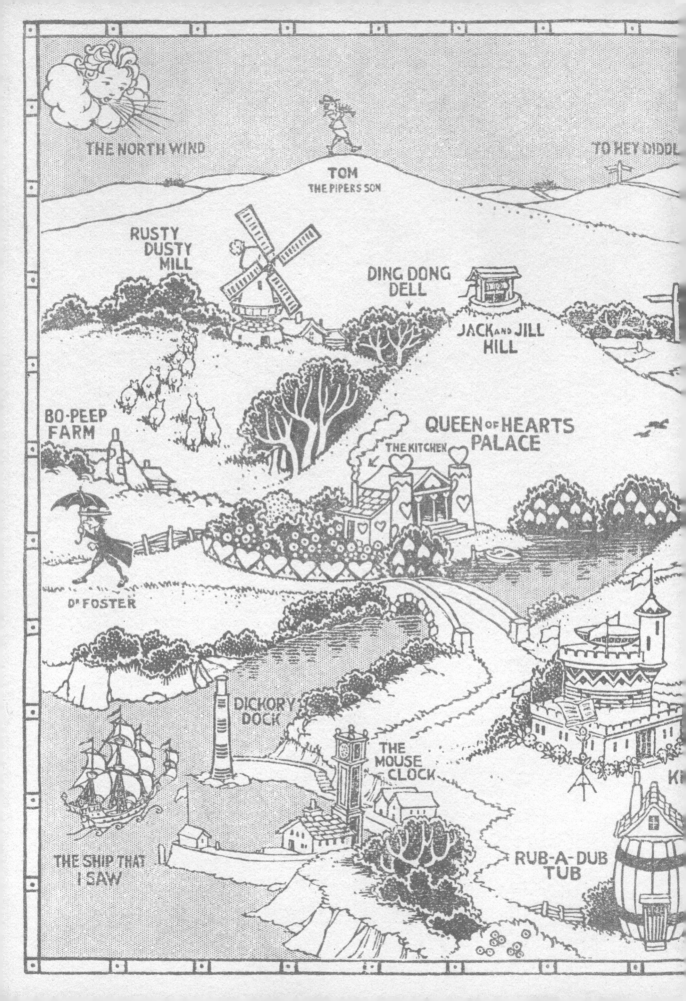